The Story of NOAH'S ARK

STORYBOOK AND WALL CLINGS

written by Lori C. Froeb
illustrated by Luana Rinaldo

I0809721

Kregel KidZone

Noah was a man who loved God very much—and God loved him. The rest of the people on Earth had forgotten about God and this made Him sad.

He told Noah to build a big boat—an ark—that could fit two of every animal and Noah's family. God was sending a flood.

When the ark was finished, Noah and his wife welcomed the animals. God sent them two by two—tigers, birds, mice, and camels.

Big and small, every kind of animal came. Noah helped them all board the boat and noticed clouds appearing in the blue sky.

As the last of the animals crawled onto the ark, Noah noticed the very first drops of rain starting to fall. Noah and his family went into the ark and God shut the door. That's when it started raining hard!

The ark began to rock as the water got deeper, and soon the ark was floating on the ocean of rain. Inside, it was warm and every animal had a place to stay. Noah took good care of the animals and made sure that they all had food to eat and water to drink.

The rain fell for 40 days and 40 nights. Thunder boomed outside and lightning lit up the sky. The animals didn't understand what was happening, but Noah and

his wife comforted them and reminded them that God would keep them safe inside the ark.

The rain finally stopped and the sun appeared in the sky. Very slowly, the water started to disappear. Noah sent out a dove to find land.

When the dove returned with a branch, Noah knew that she had found dry ground. It was time to leave the ark!

Bump! As the water dried up, the ark rested on a mountaintop. Noah opened the door and the animals crawled, ran, scurried, and flew out of the boat.

Noah and his wife looked around and smiled at what they saw.

God had put a rainbow in the sky as a sign that he would never flood the Earth again. Noah and wife praised and thanked God for keeping them all safe just as He had promised.